SAPPHOPUNK

how Sappho almost became a stone femme

a fiction in honor of otherness
an experiment in dignity

or

Sappho's queer biography

j/j hastain

Spuyten Duyvil   New York City

Acknowledgements

Thanks to T Thilleman for emotional and edits-assistance with this book. Thanks to the following journals and small presses where subsections of this work have appeared (or are forthcoming): Berfrois, Plath Profiles. Thanks to PCA and the Star House land for various somatic overlaps. The photo was taken at Rebel Salon on 39th and Tennyson in Denver.

copyright ©2015 j/j hastain

ISBN 978-1-941550-39-7

Library of Congress Cataloging-in-Publication Data

Hastain, J/J (Julia J.)
Sapphopunk : how Sappho almost became a stone femme a fiction in honor of otherness an experiment in dignity, or, Sappho's queer biography / j/j hastain.
pages cm
ISBN 978-1-941550-39-7
1. Sappho--Poetry. I. Title. II. Title: Sappho's queer biography.
PS3608.A8614S27 2015
811'.6--dc23
2014049960

*This book is dedicated to all of the dying bees
(butch martyrs like Joan of Arc, included).
This story is an eros-based complexity meant to be put
right up next to colony collapse for comparison
and
sensuous computations.*

Dear Sappho,

We have traveled together for a very long time. I feel like I can say that I *know* you (by historical implication and by intuition), but I won't say that if you don't want me to. I am positive that you *know* me. Ephemeral proximity (as ours is) leaves me no choice but to be frank (no, not the *guy*, the quality): what were you really doing at that academy? Getting drunk on unconditional love and unconditional light? Were you topping women? Were you applying a torque to where you thought they might end up: in a convention that belittled them (like you with your very own husband Cercylas)? Could it be that you were also establishing an unconditionally singing place in which your sweet daughter, Cleis, could one day grow old, subsumed in community as soul-sumptuousness (in the case of your unfortunate death)?

Devotion to the cult of Aphrodite makes sense for any priest or priestess. Content and devotion could only ever assist in expansions of the attributes that are squelched by attributed gender. A woman who engages continuance by authentic and non-automated countenance changes *that woman's* world, changes the world for all women. Of course it does not hurt to have the site of your devotion (Aphrodite) inclined toward *you* (you yourself, and the you of your students) due to the fact that you too are nubile, intensely desirable and invested in making these handmade vestments in Aphrodite's honor. Your divine (Aphrodite) is pleased with how gallant you are with the pussy-gore. Dependent on the similitude of women to her own form, Aphrodite projects herself onto the bodies of devotees as a way to see and feel herself differently by way of them. Aphrodite is a sensuous hoarder. She lives vicariously through your form, through the forms of your women.

When I tell you that I now know that you have come to visit (haunt) me so many times because you have always intended for *me* to be one of the ones to passionately sing *your* lyric, I mean that I won't call in the chorus as a way of trying to add light to your bittersweet fragments. I will, however, work for you as the women at your academy worked for you; I will personify the lushness of their loyalty. I will turn myself into a ravenous devotee and alter fulmination in hopes of delighting the not-yet-explored-enough queerness of your yearning, colorful bust.

I vow to you, I will *punk* your myth.

Deliberate gluttony is punk-aesthetics' charm. I knowingly replace lids with an eternal libido, with a randy riotous reach that renders all (who are in proximity to it) into the lengthy gulp of your myths' reverb. This is how punk-relevancies are made.

Wings are being read as they are being spread like thighs. It is possible to read a body without knowing how to read the words that might be used to describe it. Inscribe by presence. Functional utopia could never have been accurately imagined prior to it being accurately lived. There are bird wings and bee wings stored in a liquid plot. Bird wings and bee wings: wings to cover the women, the dear students.

Wings do not cover over them, but are thick with them, holding, enwrapping. Wings *with*: think of a cloak, a rhythmic grandeur. Think of linen inverting all slenderness for the sake of unearthing into form, the long gnaw of not-yet-materialized, unconditional splendor.

S begins *talking* by taking off her robes; sometimes removals of secondary skins are an actual language, a way to communicate: take off the linens (take off a skin) and an impassioned term arises on the terminus. This sensory term can nourish the team: body moderating the words, body as commissure-cleave.

A few of the young women snicker (not in a making fun of kind of way, but in a bashful way) as they look to S again and again. She looks so beautiful in the light today: part sculpture, part sculptor. They know S is the *over-soul* of this place: its breathing walls, its ardor-articulating fountains, the glass globes that dangle to reflect and refract moving light. The students feel the imprints S' fingers leave on them each time she touches them, cresting cambers and themes into their personal space.

In S's case and in the case of her girls, over-soul is another word for infinitely pleasurable potential: collaboratively placing pulse in new places and doing so as punk priestesses.

Special, spectral things happen in an intensely intentional place. Fire comes up from geodes; naturalization of anima.

The students have a language that they use when speaking with each other, when asking things of S. This language is a language that is kept secret anywhere outside of the academy. The language moves about them as an entity would: independent and pleated, demanding and without caveat. The academy can continually unify in this secret because it is something that they share: it is *discreet-ample*, so very quiet, rich with image and full.

As it embraces them, women pursue the azure jelly; they confide in the folding, feathery nest.

Women penetrate by psychic event, by incidents of intent and materializations of dynamism: mergers of energy. The students' hands look different than men's hands or heterosexual lovers' hands, because, in the time when they are attending the academy, their hands are inclined: phallic allies deliberately revolving as a way to evolve and dignify.

The bell rings through the open courtyards of the academy; the plants and flowers perk up as the ringing bell nourishes the students, prepares them to reconvene in the unconditionally offering gaze of their gluey guru.

Sometimes S wears robes, sometimes non-form-fitting dresses, but mostly she wears linen-dense pant suits. In the rooms where she instructs, time passes simultaneous to the changing light: never one without the other. One of the primary studies is the conjuring capacities of the relationship of mood to weather.

Whenever S *does* speak to the women, the *spoken* is *sung*.

Singing fragments is a way of increasing their fullness, giving them an opportunity at wholeness: "Amalgamations and augmentations in environment are sites from which to build temporary, yet continually-current identities." Her words are heard after her moving mouth and body are felt.

The students move from one of them nodding, to many of them nodding, together. They sweat on their dresses, shift the direction of their bodies in the open-walled room; as the light of the day changes, the women change with it. They know the sky's eternal, great, blue event.

Her women are looking at the wrinkles on S's face and hands; they are making *central similes* as care in regard to those wrinkles and the wrinkles in the linens of S' flowing, skirt-like pants.

S and her women are obsessed with wings. Any form of girth will do, but wings are preferred.

They are collected on land and brought into the academy for study. One large wing in hand, S shows her students the vulnerabilities of stature: "See how if you press down very hard into the airfoil-shape, it crumbles, bends in the power of your hands."

Some of them cringe and others gasp when S knowingly crushes the wing. Some of the women wonder if S is saying that they should always be soft. Or is she saying that she is hard? What would a surrounding form of hard look and feel like? Some of the women can't help but imagine S pressing around them in a way that would bruise them: beard their throb.

As S continues with the wing, one student makes no sound at all when this wing is smashed, when that wing is turned into a gory mobile. In fact, when S looks to this woman, S does not really see a woman, though what S sees is not at all a man either.

S thinks how what she is feeling in regard to this one would be hard to explain in words.

S knows much of the norms of men (due to her husband, other male suitors and her awareness that some of her women will leave her (the academy) to be with men) and notices that though this student seems present with the group, *she* is also very present somewhere else. At the moment that S thinks this, S feels something wrong in her having called this student "she."

There is an emotional elegance to this student, but there is also a complex, possibly concerning glint in the eye, a refusal to participate as readily as the other women. S wonders if this will be a problem for her academy, for all she has worked to build.

S notes nuances in the folds of her consideration (possibly, staring a little bit too long in the direction of that student who has too much of her attention right now), before moving back to the wing and the other women who are conducive: the wide-eyed women.

S walks by her students, whispers wordless, mouth-shapes to them as her fingers lightly graze their gazes. Her students' gazes become alert when she touches their shoulders or has her hands tangled in their hair.

S is seeding; S does not seed by rote. With no open vowels there is no moan. S responds to this belittling, outside norm by nourishing the mouth's incessant cadence: lip to ear, nose to shoulder, shudder to float, *sound*. Her students always sense S's energy as a form of simultaneity: strength and sustenance.

The young women are confident that S is what feeds their middle: the shared language.

When men outside of it ask S intellectualizing or practical questions about her academy, she often dodges the questions, squelches the inquiries. It is no man's business what she is doing in the livelihood of light with her women.

S is convinced that the men she meets will never understand the need to be held in the shape of a mirror. S is part mother, part provender and part father-provider for these women; their emancipations are personal for her. S and her women share shards, shred tenuous past lives. S does not own them (regardless of how some of the men tease S about this very thing), but she relates to them by way of an undying, primal intimacy: "They are me and I am them. We are each other's reflections as we become." She speaks these truths of hers while privately pondering her women's orgasms.

She indicates herself in a firm voice (not singing) when she is in the areas of men. She holds her own: embodies hardness. S experiences extreme relief when she finally turns her back to the cloying eyes and fidgeting, coarse hands of the probing men in the streets.

One afternoon, when she begins adding rouge flower petals to the black tea (which the women regularly steep at the school (like monks make Chartreuse liquor)) the strength of rouge being mixed begins to make the girls' eyes roll back: eye-spin by aroma and aesthetic, long before by swig.

S wants her dears to know themselves as inherent beauty even if that can only ever be known by them after the fact of study and sensation; *inborn after-the-fact* is a completely appropriate method to acquiring knowledge by embodiment: no rule books, no strings attached.

S insists that she is not making marionettes; she is enabling personified breath-shepherds and breathing their breath. The women push and S pushes back, gently, showing them that there are no limits to her offer. S is implanting skid marks in the tendencies of women to settle for allowing themselves to be shut down. S is adding bones to deboned wings.

S gets the girls drunk so that they can let go of the counter effects of their pasts, the patriarchal impositions. S wants it to be possible that they not have to spend the precious time of their studies in the academy, rehashing, and thereby reifying antiquated wounds.

"My little umbilical mages, my lambs, I will lead you but it will never be to slaughter: I promise. I have imagined so much for you. This livelihood is yours; I am all yours."

A panorama spreads; a unique style is foundational in the prospect. While with her, S wants these women to learn that they never have to leave; they are Cleis' mothers and sisters and lovers. S will forever increase fodder, spill into pounding, *be* the dominant lover that they so desperately need.

Over time the academy of S and her women is becoming a collective, functioning together in beehive-like prime. Collective: a *we*, a *they* speaking *with* each other *as* an each other. They are able to speak accurately for and on behalf of one other. It is too much to have to be the one speaking for yourself all the time, they agree. Having to be the sole progenitor of self is like relentlessly tying knot after knot in each whatnot, during an unending process of enfolding and unfolding. They are an overtime-scholarship of body, of sensations. They are a thrilling congeal, a phantasmagoria able to withstand and committed to growing a communal wish:

hone by honey.

The academy agrees about the problem of binary-derived pronouns: binary this and binary that *is* a problem in *any* historical framework. They bring in the image of a three-fold wing. Then, they look over at the student who is staring out the window during this conversation; they are threatened by the student who does not fit in and the women who fit in, cringe.

S considers. S convinces the women that though the binary is a problem, they can choose to define themselves *within her*. S will guarantee that each of them has enough space within the pronouns *she* and *her* if they so choose. S is a *her* in which accurate space for her women can be guaranteed. Without disagreement there is no real need for discussion. All of the women except *one* are invested in *she* and *her as* expansiveness.

S smiles on her dears. S worries about the one.

More than anything, the women of the academy are interested in the pungency of the breath-grammar that they are collectively producing, on which they are getting drunk; they prefer the fervent inhalations and exhalations, the feelings themselves, over the ways that words have been historically imbued. They are making their own power structure outside of patriarchy: a power structure that works for *them*.

Imbibing on the power structure that they are inventing. *Present tense, present tense.*

S continues considering the problem of the *one* student who does not give an opinion during the discussion, but whose body is held in such an erect shape, whose demeanor obviously sets them apart from the others: the one who sits in the back of the room, perspiring and painting, head shaking side to side (and not up and down in the nod that seems to be common between the other women).

S is a queer queen. Advancing the sodden arch, a land-butch invests in the landform in which she resides. Women are landforms to a land-butch: her women are the place in which S resides. These women are S' home. There is only *one* queen bee and she is fertile for the entirety of her life. S has enough fecundity within her to infinitely stimulate, since she has fed herself *royal jelly* (that of her proclivities to and consecrations of Aphrodite) since her practice began.

Practicing as *priestess of Aphrodite* has implanted, in S, an undying drive to produce and consume beauty. S likes to think that, as she consumes, she is making space for her students to neither have to be *only* worker bees (female and unable to reproduce) nor *only* stinger-less drones (potential mates of the queen (which, due to the barb in their sex organs, are guaranteed death post-mating)). She is making space in them for future resonances. S continually envisions other emotional, spiritual and physical options for the women of her academy; she conjures cooperative thrive.

From clavicle to hip curve (not necessarily extremely curvaceous hip curve: some of the women who attend S' school have rather stick-like forms, have nearly no breasts) there is a brimming core call for S to offer tender tractions to her women: to touch every aspect of every woman's body until S knows each one, one by one, by memory.

S composes songs for the beauty she consumes, pushes past contingencies in order for her to feel all of that beauty being freed here and now. Jelly is not perverse; it is gaudy gold, the combustibility of identity, the smear in the afternoon light. S strokes musculature as a form of musk, releases the bodies wordlessly, and then with the sounds, more than the logics of words.

There is parturition and blood to share; some *elementals* (as S is training these women to be) need to be held in jelly as they recombine with the living, post the many stages of their own rot.

S is land-butch-viviparous: contiguously expanding her own boundaries as a way to honor how much she longs to hold the wealth of the whole expanding unit inside of her.

Stone fruits decay when they are kept in storage; the academy is a version of storage that S is constantly aerating, experimenting with, recommitting to, living off of. Plums, avocados, nectarines, apricots, peaches, cherries and hybrid fruits are all susceptible to rhizopus rot. S prefers to offer her students the experience of *soft rot* (as rhizopus rot is) over the experience of hard rot: something in the embodiment of the former allows S to safeguard and ensure. Ensuring is what these women need.

Aromatic lesions are a sign that the process is going as planned. The rot has to arise in order for S to be able to attend to it. She wants her women to rot in the present tense. This is one of the reasons that S discourages the flourish of antiquated wounds at her academy; she wants these women, this beauty, to know what *else* it can be by way of her.

Sometime S' students wake with wafting, watery, chocolate-colored marks on their skin. S' hands are soaked in the vibrant, vibrating bouquet of these marks.

Consider the difference between the womb's value in its historicity of heterosexual *use* (e.g.: childbearing) and the womb as absolute, limitless, personal portal.

S encourages the students to consider their own bodies (her body) as they make paper maché honeycombs. "You can put all of your trinkets and talismans in the center. Thoughtful placement of them can be a way of making *your things* cling to you. You can *mark* what you are on your *mass* every day. You can progress your evolution from within you. I will provide graphite pencils, utensils. I vow to Aphrodite that I will enable you."

Sharing in the act of scribing generates syzygy, erogenous bondage.

"I make it out of my own flesh: self-made character as path. You don't need caricature here," S mutters, transmuting migrations through her *thiasos* by confessional chant. The women watch as they drag their own fingers over the forming stretch marks on their bellies, as they extend their curious (not probing) fingers toward S' own engraved, bare belly. Womb etchings make the pillows back in their dimly lit and awaiting, wall-less rooms, wet.

This is usually the time when S chooses a lover, takes a stronghold around the young woman's hand (as the other women look on with awe, await eagerly), lifts her and leads her into the ceremonial chamber with intent to feed her enough royal jelly that this dear woman's body froths into furthermore.

S' breasts are small but her stance is varied and wide: inclusive. The young woman whom S has chosen, willingly begins to close her eyes to S' insistence, but before this student closes eyes completely, she mouths to S (but makes no sound): "Your hair is so beautiful pinned back like that. You look so strong. You are everything I have ever dreamed of. You touch me so deeply. I need you. I trust you. I shall be ever maiden for you."

S ties the young woman's hands while singing the words "my muse with beautiful hair" into this woman's open mouth. The caress between them could be called hand sex, the indelible eros of the inner thigh, pelvis as location of a mutual centripetal pride. The velvet impact takes place and it is perfect, just perfect.

The young woman is thinking how this is like sleeping with her eyes open. She can't wait to tell her fellow students how this feels! She weeps at how pronounced she is becoming in the shapeliness of S' physiological proclamation: a dulcimer-like descant occurring within this woman's own body.

Afterward, the altered woman must find her way up the lenient ladder, blindfolded. When she arrives on the uppermost level of the ceremonial chamber, S is there to greet her and offer her drenched fruit. There is music. It is not cliché to sing of the sensuous discharges that fruit enables in the bodies that are susceptible to its juices. When the young woman takes a bite, S sees her eyes filling with S. That bite turns fruit into carnage within the body. S sees the student's maw change into something predatory at the moment of this threshold crossing. This is S' favorite part: when the women show themselves, intentionally or unintentionally, as animals.

"This is the other side of the perception: the permeation that arises after sensuous steering," S thinks to herself, and bows her head to the image of Aphrodite that she now sees projected over the voluptuous embodiment of this student regardless of whether or not the woman's body, is, in fact, voluptuous.

The student is wobbling as S steers them both back the group. S knows she needs a constant presence of sex in order for her to feel stable. "A wise woman uses what she needs, and not merely what she has been given, in order to balance herself. Needs abound here: prominent and obvious needs, subtle and subliminal needs. <u>Beat your breasts girls, tear your tunics.</u>"

There is an unexpected and abrupt grunt from the student who continually sets themselves apart, and the swagger in that sound interrupts the high on which the women are sharing a ride. The same student who had initially caught S' attention for a little bit too long a few weeks prior, is becoming increasingly disruptive. S gets nervous at the sound of the grunt (nervousness is uncharacteristic of her).

Perhaps S is just tired from topping that other woman as she just had; she really does give them her *all*, her heart of insatiable longing, each of them, one by one.

S slowly raises her eyes to meet the eyes of whom she has come to refer (privately) as *my outcast*. The student peers directly into S (indoors the fire is kindled). None of her other students ever peer directly into her in that way; they lovingly avert their eyes.

"What makes you think that what you are doing here will balance me?" this *one* challenges.

Sometimes that is all it takes: the speech and surprising, stimulating push of one.

An adrenaline rush shoves its way through the room and is perceptible to the women as a sudden, frightening anxiety. It has been so long since any of them has felt dissention (having long left the trials and expectations of family-life, and quotidian imposition and gender roles behind), that their loose and willing bodies tighten as if they have been seared internally by something *outside*.

The scattering scar sups the most curvaceous side of the honeycomb and the students begin to suppurate.

S tucks in each of her students. When she begins to hear that they are settling in for the night (the collective rise and fall of the academy's shared *breath grammar*), S retires, alone, to her room and opens her womb-opus to Aphrodite. It begins: "I spoke to you, Aphrodite, in a dream."

Once the portal starts to yawn, Aphrodite speaks urgently (as if she has been waiting *too long*): "You are my servant Eros. The profession of *possession* is difficult. My love, I can see that something is weighing on you."

As is customary for this ritual, S picks up her gold-tipped hammer and slams it down on her first finger. Blood shoots, internally, from belly to brain. Blood gathers under the chitin of the nail.

"It is my outcast, dear one. I know not how to reach her; I know not whether I should even call this bud *her*." Another slam of hammer to the next finger on the hand: "I can see the desire, I sense the drive, but I know not how to court it." The conversation continues until every finger on S' hand is empurpled: red blood, then with time, black.

S considers weeping at the sensation, but then decides that since it is not tears that get Aphrodite's attention she should perform something that actually makes her more vulnerable to Aphrodite than tears do.

It is S, in vulnerable positions, that gets and keeps Aphrodite's attention.

Tearless, with blood beginning to brim and spill out from beneath her fingernails, S considers a lace-like liberation, thinks of a rainbow moving from seemingly present, to dripping, due to what surrounds it, what compels it. S ponders the complexities of royal jelly, meditates on how the ordinary becomes divine.

What forms of pollen-sentimentalism will she feed her students tomorrow? How will she bring them back from the fear that S' one, S' outcast, had made in them in their own specialized space? Royal jelly is part chemical, part milk and part mystery. It has the power to reduce scarring, hasten catalytic feat, and stimulate cell-salvage.

S feels herself exhaling, calmed and fusing with the throbbing beneath her nails.

Then, interruption of her own exhale, paranoia, a jolt, "But how am *I* to be *causality* of a form of royal jelly that will, in fact, reach my outcast? Am I capable of that? What would that even look like?"

The form in which S usually distributes royal jelly (by topping her students) may not be enough in this case, S thinks, but can think of no other shapely replacement for what she has practiced at the academy for so many years.

Mid-panic and without the relief of synthesis, S falls asleep.

Pomegranates are rolling in a roiling and vivacious tide. Pomegranates, like poem fragments, protrude from the curls and tugs prior to them being shoved back into the expanse of the larger body of water. As S wades toward the pomegranates, caught in the agitation of the curl, she notices that no matter the distance it seems like she has gone in pursuit of them, she never even gets near the tide cycles.

Her hair is turning gray; pieces of it are falling out. It is not until she gives up on what she realizes as her past method and turns herself over to the expanse of the sea *in abandon,* weeping wildly (mixing herself with the expanse's contents in a hysterical way (that is very unlike how she ever is with her students or Aphrodite)), that she notices the pomegranates that are actually bobbing and floating right near her: graspable, proximate.

Is S a synesthesiac-synergy leading her devotees to carnal and cosmic ease, into unconditional spring?

Plainly, S is aware of <u>power and beauty and knowledge:</u> the <u>threefold in wonder.</u> S will begin to open herself to new approaches, shifts in structure. S knows that she does not have it within her to leave any of her students behind: those proximate, nor those far off.

S understands that one form of near is a form of far and that one form of far, is an unforeseen form of near.

It seems to her that the complexities of the outcast (that S cannot interact with that student *as a woman*) cannot be simplified by the mere fact that S wants so desperately to *touch*, to *include*.

What if the outcast does not *want* to be touched? Could that even be possible? "What woman would not want to be topped by me!" S states: not really a question as she regards the one who really seems not to be referred to as a woman. S knows Aphrodite prospers when S expresses confidence, so S tries to express confidence whenever she can find it within her.

Why is the outcast even here at all then? Had they misinterpreted the rumors that they heard about the academy?

"You come here to be possessed, to be taken, to be remade: recombinant dyad." Students willingly come to S' academy to commit to their perspectives being cubed, to oblige pairing.

Does the outcast expect something from their experience at the academy that S is unable to provide?

"What am I unable to provide?"

S wonders. Instead of S answering her own question, as is customary for S, it is Aphrodite who answers.

After nights of commune with Aphrodite and days of commune with her students, S wakes and gathers only some of her things (she likes to leave some of her things behind when she travels, she likes to approach travel *from behind*, does this in order to put herself in a vulnerable state; Aphrodite attends to S when she is in vulnerable states): a pants-suit made of purple linen, the leathery skin of a dead frog (which reminds her of a crura), a gold-bound pipe, a loaf of wheat-bread cut in half and daubed with honey on its middle, a garland recently made for her by her students.

There are favored things that S chooses to leave behind: her mobile altar, the dried roses and incense ash that are mixed in her golden cup, beech-wood sound instruments, gems in a chest that was fashioned out of piles of driftwood from the shore, her favorite girdle.

S knows she needs to bring Cleis a gift; her daughter is *bold spice* and will be expecting some lush and grandiose performance of S' love. Though, S often cautions Cleis about tears of grief (and how those tears are unbecoming (that they do not get Aphrodite's attention)), she also admires the strength that Cleis seems to articulate on her own. Sometimes she thinks that Cleis prefers to move about her life without calling Aphrodite in; this concerns S, and (covertly), this impresses S.

S will bring Cleis a vial of perfume, a gathering of vetch, and a few oil-stained scrolls: intoxicating and maternal aroma to replace so much of the role of mother (to Cleis), for which S has been stealth.

Whenever S leaves the academy, one or more of her students hold space for her until she returns. The premise that the women of the academy have agreed upon is that whomever feels called to, can take up S' form in whatever shapely honor they might imagine for themselves, for her.

Sometimes wings are held up to the light so that the light can freely shine through them. Other approaches involve securing the wings to their backs and moving about the academy as lightly as possible, even with that additional wing-weight.

"Move into a holding shape that would make her most know that we adore her," one of them says, while shifting the direction she is facing so that more of her bare, smooth skin is facing the sun.

Sometimes the young women hold the same shape that S holds in the statue recently founded in her honor (in Syracuse). As they *act* like S' statue *looks,* they hold her with them, while simultaneously trying not to tie her down to only one place. As they do this, some of the women close their eyes to the sun that they are facing; the women wait.

They feel S' jelly in them when the sun shines directly onto their closed eyes. They wake in the morning with burned eyelids. The women will do anything to be close to her: her stature, her countenance, the weight that she offers them when she is holding them down by towering over them during initiation rituals.

They miss her sensual cognizance. They are *embodied epithalamia*, dripping in her absence.

Some of the students miss S so much that they border on hysteria while she is away. They feel that the academy is dying without her physical presence and her singing discourses. They see the flowers go limp, the garlands begin to crisp. Retiring to their beds early and refusing to eat, they are viscerally jealous of the attention that Cleis is getting and they use that jealousy as a sensation to lead them into sleep.

This era of lack is the only time that these women dream and recall their dreams. Are all shadows the fascia by which dream states are entered and retained? While they agree with the premise that S' academy should be a place where women can experience the eros and endogenous fanfare of the particular quality of *safe space* that S creates, the women can't help but try to use their minds and her words to rush her back to them: "let thy strong spirit never fear," on spoken-sung-repeat, hour after hour.

When it has been too long, the women begin to ramble and blab; they even try to use the language of the townsmen, cursing, being crass, knowing S would not approve. They do this to show her that they need her as their teacher and their lover, to try and draw her back earlier than she might have planned. They do this until they hear the bell marking her return from her travels.

The embankments surrounding the academy are filled with mobile altars wafting S' favorite incenses. Abounding cairns-stacks of un-cracked and cracked geodes that have been dipped in these womens' menstrual blood, stand high. Large wings are propped like chairs with billowy fabric wads in them for pillows. Perfumes are being poured into the soil.

As S comes into contact with the women, they wipe aromatic unguents on her skin; they wipe their hands along the sides of her pinned-back hair.

Once S has opened her arms to each woman she is relieved: her intuited species is still intact.

S divines Aphrodite as intercessory between the women and her in order to keep *commune fluency*. One of S' students relays to her that the whole time she has been away, Phaon (the confrontational *one*, the outcast) has *also* been away.

"When we were doing the statue ritual, *she* just jumped the fence before we could even get to *her* and protest."

Sing-songy: "Oh honey, it's probably best not to call Phaon *she* or *her*, but thanks for telling me. Where is Phaon now?"

Ever since S heard the name (a few weeks prior to her leaving to visit Cleis) she remained unable to get it out of her mouth; the name drenches her tongue like the fruit she offers them drenches the tongues of her students.

S secures her women by way of particular address of *particular* forms of decay. The decay she prefers is so somatic and real that it refutes all forms of decoy, drenching the always softening parts of the stone fruit, her women. *Turning on* the temporary predator within each one of them, S serves; one form of rot can become another form of rot, each of them, soft.

Followed by her devotees, who trail in a curved, gown-like shape, S turns a corner.

She sees that the women of the academy have created paper maché baths, outdoors, <u>in the gray olive-grove</u>. In each bath, an individual woman's paper maché honeycomb floats, and the baths, while holding water, also continually leak. Leaking entrails of wetness are conduits: from where the women are to where they are going. Elegant sails, removed from their masts, are folded and tucked in order that they are capable of being filled in an upside down fashion: filled up by pressure and not by penetration.

The women, in the academy, strip bare and climb into their individual, deep tubs. Without prompting it through words, they move *with* one another. This is the grace of the honey. Holding their breaths, they submerge all at once and once they are fully submerged, each of them uses their hands delicately, turning themselves upside down.

In the process of hopping over the fence, Phaon snags burlap pants on the wooden slats of the academy fence. This wood has been made sharp by weather. From where Phaon is, straddling the fence, they can see how beautiful the female form is when it overfills the liquid of a leaking containment by way of its weight.

"Women belong in hand-made baths," Phaon thinks, vividly. Well, the thought *is* vivid! Phaon ponders how the human body is mostly water. Then, once that thought has passed, Phaon looks across the numerous baths to try and find the one that S is in.

Phaon wants to locate S, personally, before S and the women's breath-grammar obscures S' view of Phaon.

As Phaon finds S, the rush in their *stone* returns.

Phaon has not felt that since the last time that S was near Phaon's physical body. Exaggerated masculinity? Always. But floods in the physiologically-irrelevant-yet-totally-extant and irreverent dick? That seems to currently be S-dependent.

Phaon's dick is not only below the belt but is in Phaon's whole body: voice too.

Phaon has felt tortured by S' seeming refusal to be a stone femme. Phaon has been contemplating this for months. Of course Phaon does not *know* that she won't be, but has gathered as much from watching S intently with her women.

"Why do physical genitals have to matter so much if there is so much *more* that I can do with the salience of my *actual* (whole body) dick?

Though it plagues, Phaon keeps this wondering to themself. As S rises, upright and naked in the bath in the middle of the courtyard, Phaon experiences the full body rush that they know to be their erection, once again.

Before letting any of the women at the academy see Phaon watching them, Phaon is ensuring Aphrodite that the one who tops (S), *will* be topped.

"I will call her Psappha. I will take her by implanting in her own sentiments while she is living them." After the words, Phaon sends the idea directly into Aphrodite, "This will be a ritual offered *to* S by *me*. There is no room for you in what I am going to do, so stay out of it."

Phaon remembers the first time Aphrodite was near: how Phaon sensed a trickster in her. Phaon offers her passage by boat nonetheless: any *gentleman* would. At first, there is that whole body rush (erection) in response to Aphrodite's physical beauty, but then, in response to her unforeseen shape shift, Phaon goes totally limp. "<u>Stand up and look at me, face to face,</u>" Phaon hassles the crone. What they feel from her in response to *demand*, is not activity or reverberation at all, but submissiveness: a low and relentless drone.

Weeks of lyre-playing and meter training in outdoor scenes reestablishes the circadian-in-stretch: the tempo of tide and pour in the academy.

S has been less able to find Aphrodite in her personal, womb-based portal rituals lately. She wonders why. There is no one to whom she can tell this fact, but Phaon has been staring intently at her since her return. S wonders if she can confide in Phaon regarding this one thing.

"Phaon is, in fact, different than my other women," S thinks. But instead of confiding, S absorbs Phaon's regular regard and continues on independently, struggling.

She feels Aphrodite close enough that she knows she has not been abandoned by her, but she also feels a sophisticated rift between her divine and herself. Sometimes Aphrodite implants these rifts for the sake of teaching S how to expand, so S does not confront Aphrodite about what she is currently sensing.

S knows that she is responsible for nursing cosmic archetypes by way of her own body. Beauty's project is to swallow onlookers. Knowing this, S gawps and glowers into the rifts: treats the difficulty as her duty. She wants to forever earn her right to Aphrodite. S is willing to be a <u>voice virgin</u>, an acquiescent, yet highly-faithful nubile, for as long as it takes.

Alone in her room, S whispers into the incense as it wafts from her altar.

"Spirit is activation of the volition-ridden tangibles of my *me*. Spirit is the parts of me that are me, but perhaps are not yet inside of me or are not yet being embodied *by* me. I feel myself entirely as spirit, lately. <u>Hour by hour I sit</u>. Where is my susurrating body? Where is my ability to transduce, to gulp the grief of women, their pasts, so that they have more space in them to consider their own *elses*?

Embodiment of spirit as an activism which activates body, is my sense of place: the place I have made for myself in the world. We aren't born women, we turn ourselves into the women that we are."

Unsure if she is preparing for a more formal form of contact with her students, S continues to wander, part sing-song, part direct speech like she uses in the streets when talking to the men: both out loud.

Something is changing. S feels it pierce.

Unable to get Phaon's insistent watching of her out of her spirit, her swaying body, or her attire, S wonders if she should leave the academy again. There are, of course, other towns that wish her to visit. She could cultivate more women there. She could even visit her husband if she needed an excuse. But what about her students? Would she be abandoning them if she left? Leaving them like she hopes Aphrodite is not leaving her?

"No, I can't abandon the hive."

But what to do with these feelings pushing her toward Phaon?

Honey: sticky, never texturally precise. Honey: clear as mud.

S excuses herself early from study again and the students, who have been wondering and worrying, are now sure of it: something is severely troubling S. They sense it physically, when she is experiencing feelings that take her from them in any way. They feel the light of their bodies begin to crumble; their wings curdle inward. It is during this crumbling that they feel, somatically, what a surrogate S is for them: their joy is dependent on the join.

A tendril-telepathy had to be built in the academy early on, in order to ensure that the sinew and connective tissue always remained there for the women to engorge upon. Though technically being temporarily trained in tendril-therapy and the erotic arts (which some of them eventually put to use with their husbands when they leave the academy), students at the academy never really have to leave. The invitation is not short term. S makes an unconditionally, all-encompassing, sultry cosmos for them: magnetizing them forever inward, toward the center of the hive.

With S, they are guaranteed linking union with each other, with each wing and petal on academy grounds and, most importantly, with the center of the shared language: *their* S.

Like normal, Phaon has placed self at a distance from the other women at the academy. As the women sit in the flowers they talk about how they think *she* is a snob (S has asked them to stop referring to Phaon as *she*).

"She is intentionally, emotionally unavailable," they gripe. The women are angry.

Phaon sits in the bare dirt, where there are no flowers, and is thinking about how, by having become familiar with the way that S has previously taught, Phaon can now see that S is unconditionally conducive to something *other than* how she has operated in the past.

S is conducive to splits, to splitting, to nuance-based shadow sides. Can S feel Phaon's thoughts about her as vitalizing penetrations by way of this pointed pheromone-transfer? Phaon hopes so; Phaon is asserting. If this hope is in fact true, then it would at least be a beginning to what Phaon has known needs to happen.

Can S feel this opening-further of potential? Can *this* potential, drive divergent forms of transcendence? Can S conceive of a reason to transcend the anatomy of her academy? S offers her students their own *elses*, but is she too embedded in and wed to what she has built to even consider what *else* for her?

Phaon picks contemplating-stone-self up from the soft soil and soil sticks to the open palms (which are used for standing leverage). Phaon has decided that there has been enough waiting. Walking right past the bickering women, Phaon nears S' closed door. The bickering women roll eyes and quaff.

Before entering, Phaon places an open, dirty palm on the door knob and opens eyes to sky, as dripping warmth becomes drenched storm. Phaon prefers the numinous nature of awash; Phaon is missing their ship's sway in the sea just like S's women are missing S' sway. Phaon commits to their ship: "My caress will be near you again, my love, my immeasurable mate."

Though it is closed, S' door is unlocked. As Phaon is getting ready to turn the knob, S turns it from inside of her room. Her room is different than the chamber in which S initiates her students by eros, sanguinity and sex.

Phaon has never been in either place; Phaon is *so* other.

First realization upon entry: S' fingers are red, black. It looks like paint is dripping from the maximum of her. Phaon loves paint, but wonders how it got there, on S' hands? When Phaon computes what is going on, there is the realization that the color on S' lips, table, fingertips, is from her own leaking.

She is beautiful: a half-cracked geode dipped in blood, a probable-meme for stone femme.

"I want so desperately to hold them up." Moaning extension: "I want to let them know that they never have to leave. Some of them will leave; some of them will always leave. Do their awaiting weddings have that much clout?"

Phaon remains quiet, but listens, eyes acute and arms slowly expanding to encircle S while she is speaking. Phaon's middle is growing too. Phaon notices that S is not singing these words. This is something that she never shows the students.

"I have called on Aphrodite for many days consecutively now. She is still not responding. <u>I am an inch from dying</u>. For a while I waited in her honor, but I need her too much to wait any longer. For the life of me, I don't understand why she won't respond to me. I have been pounding and drowning on my blood for days."

Phaon knows that Aphrodite's *aloof* has come from Phaon's own demand of her in regard to Phaon's next step.

S breaks from Phaon's slowly tightening arms and erect middle, returns her hand to the wooden altar table, which is already covered in her secretions. The gold head of the hammer nearly slams down again on S' frigid form, before Phaon even understands that this bleeding has come by S' own hand!

Phaon grunts a bit in the pocket of time between the realization and when Phaon can actually get to S, to muscle the hammer from her grip. Phaon stops her from continuing to crush in the name of a divinity that is not even currently present with her.

It is the suddenness and brusqueness of Phaon's grip on her arm (possibly leaving a bruise, causing her to release the hammer from her own strong grip) that not only get S' attention, but changes it.

Phaon pushes S against the paper maché wall that is lit by candlelight from behind it. S has been making the paper wall for many years now, privately, in her own room. The wall flexes to account for their shared heft. The breathing wall is receptive to their weight: takes responsibility for them.

S shakes in Phaon's clasp. S notes the command in the poise of the shape that is obviously about to possess her: engorged and firm. She has only ever been possessed by Aphrodite for these many years. The standard: Aphrodite is to S what S is to her women. The candlelight in the room rushes to dark. S' knees buckle and she faints, but she does not hit the floor.

Phaon catches her.

Stone butches are not susceptible like stone fruits are. Stone butches don't rot and change in the present tense like stone fruits do.

As a stone butch, Phaon's sexual pleasure and sexual releases come from arousal and facilitation of *bustle* in Phaon's lovers' genitals. S wakes to Phaon stroking her head, "Psappha, Psappha," then her small, tight breast, "Psappha Psappha," then further.

S interrupts by reaching up and pulling Phaon's face into her, shoving facial bones against her chest; S almost breaks them: hard facial bones to not-very-breasted-chest. As they tangle, they simulate a large hourglass full of hair.

No matter what way the hour or the glass is flipped, an enjoined *inter* remains there, arced and stable.

S realizes that, for a few moments, here, as she is directed by Phaon's hand, she is not thinking about Aphrodite.

"The bodily pleasure and the salt is so much it is taking all of my attention!" What a relief, she thinks. A stone butch sailor is a code. Phaon's gaze and grip-based regard indicates how a stone butch's consideration of a woman's body is so much different than a land butch's is.

Land butch leaves some space in the assertion for rest; stone butch, a constant stimulation, and a stone butch lover's mammilla is *kept* on point.

At a distance, Aphrodite grits her teeth, clamps her hands so hard that if she had a human form they would cramp.

"Musk by *purge*: purge is for replacing *purgatory*," she says out loud. "You have to work for it Sappho! Amorousness is passion and moves with *me*; where I go it goes. It does not go where you go just because you are there. You are not divine without me."

She loves S' finger-crushing ritual; it gives Aphrodite ripening sensations in her glands, turns them into fruit. "You burn for me and only me," jealous intoning. "She will come back to me. She always does." Aphrodite points this phrase in S' direction and as she scans S' body in the throes of ardent delight, Aphrodite quakes.

S is on her back and Phaon is topping her, tapping into her most lurid growl.

Somewhere, a fable is coming unthreaded; an embodied beehive explodes in the stormy air. Name it: flicker-infinitum in the matching of desires that they share across genders.

Averting the eyes is one way of progressing, but to do so, bypasses even the momentary possibility of burning in a stone butch's living *give*. To be an incarnate hinge, dependent on variant sensations, means that those sensations might just *taproot* you, transplant you altogether from where you were to where you might choose to go from here.

S does not remember the last time she felt wide-eyed. S' wide-open eyes are like gooseneck barnacles oozing sperm. Phaon is giving S a different kind of jelly: kingly kink.

Lubrication, then elongation of a hasty, aggressive nature gives way to eventual unforeseen expanse. Enter the body of another. Phaon's hands are within S but they are not only approximations or phallic allies (as S had taught her students that their hands can be).

Phaon's hand *is* phallus: this one and that one. This one and that one make a balance in S' burgeoning body.

How had she not sensed this in her, in so many years of work with her students? How had she missed this pivotal place so in need of pronouncement? Is it possible to discourage the internal presence of multiple portals due to your limiting focus on only one tactic?

There is wine on the table near the altar and it rocks on the table, spilling in the stunning wake of their force: this labor. Their rocking is folding them; fold is indelible sate.

As she nears it, S thinks that her own orgasm might be the only supple tenacity applicable to the living code of a hunting stone butch. She sings it to Phaon: "Orgasm is the geode's geode."

Phaon pulls out a notebook and places it on the bed near where S is still sleeping. She came hard: harder than Phaon has ever felt a lover cum. Is this hard rot? Can S respond to hard rot when in the grip of a stone butch? Blood is still encrusted on the insides of S' thighs.

Hours pass before S wakes to the mid-day light and opens the notebook. She opens the book, still high on the aesthetic and poise of Phaon. S goes directly to the book before even wondering on the potentially wandering state of her students during her abnormally lengthy absence.

Hand written:

"Sappho,

I left this for you because I want you to know that, though I am leaving, I am not leaving *you*. We have contoured the verve of this verb now; we have made each other elegant.

Behind this letter you will find some of the paintings that I completed while at your academy. Even though it is uncharacteristic of me to admit it, I was paying a lot of attention to you, to your women, to the way that you are *with* your women. I felt so much while I was here.

I often dreamed of all of you during the few times I jumped the fence to return to my ship, and, when I dream, I paint. The whole side of my ship is covered in murals. Maybe I will be able to come back one day and if I do I will take you to my ship; I will show you. My ship is my body. I often dye my sails relevant colors as matter for relating.

After looking these paintings over myself, I am sure that you should have each of them (three for your women, one for you, and one *of* me). They touch on the surreality of your self-made sororale; they show my appreciation of your competence.

Please Psappha, let these lead you to a more demand-based relationship with Aphrodite. You are as powerful as she is, even if she would prefer you not know it. She should be prostrate to you as much as you are prostrate to her. You really do quench women's clenches and it was my pleasure to quench you."

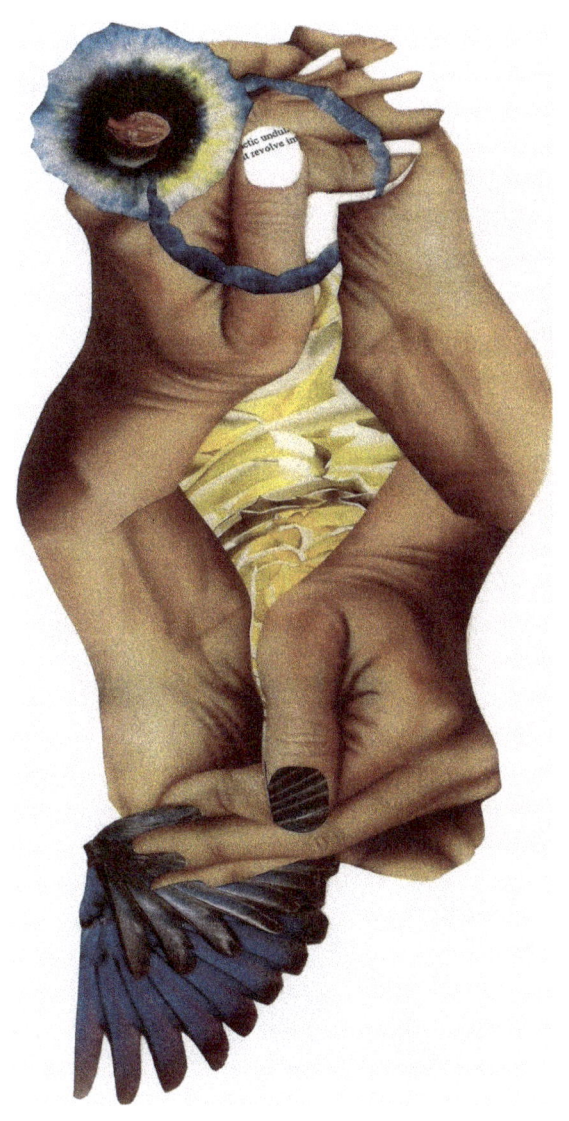

A stone butch lover paints the sails of their boat red in order to announce that, though the passion and drive are *true*, follow-through was the prerogative. Longevity is just not possible; the need to leave challenges the intensity of the particular feeling.

In this sun, the sun to which Phaon will bow, Phaon's body still shimmers from the shape-shifting crone's ointment. Curly locks are glowing as they wave in the sea breeze; a whole body leans, like a spear on the phallic spar.

"Phaon, O my lover! Don't leave me!" S shouts after she has flipped through the pages of Phaon's notebook, soaked in the images of Phaon's feeling.

The paintings are so intense that she feels that they make S' aura ache. She runs beyond the perimeter of the academy; her women are watching, shocked by S' erratic behavior. *What is going on here?* The looks on their faces articulate their confusion.

Pursuing the mythical boatman, S sweats until she reaches the cliff's edge. She tests it toe-by-toe, trying with all of her vigor to see Phaon. She fears her will can't take her far enough out this time; she's not prone to out!

She can only see the back of Phaon's waving strands like little, ruddy locks in the sea breeze. She can't see the front of Phaon at all. More than three-fourths of her body is leaning over the edge, and as she struggles, she weeps.

The red sails are certainly indicative of the mystical boatman's care of her, but S is staring even beyond them, looking for that poise unique to Phaon. As Phaon's boat leaves Lesbos and the academy, Phaon *is* leaving S.

"How could Phaon not know that I *am* this place?"

Aphrodite knows S for her bold embodiment, her steadiness, her imaginative action and her inclusivity of women. Not wanting S to be lost to an unfortunate death, now that Phaon (and the power Phaon has over Aphrodite) has left, Aphrodite sweeps in.

S makes the raucous and unrefined sound of a wounded animal. The sound catches in her cells.

"This wound will hurt forever. It will always be active, never be antiquated. This will always assert itself in me. I will never rid myself of it."

In this awareness, S understands that it was, perhaps, an antiquated attitude in her, a blind bend to Aphrodite's pressure, that made her make her students' antiquated wounds disappear from them, previously. S sees that her doing that, takes away some of the power of their memory.

S chokes on the welling whale inside of her: the wail which, in all of this writhing, just might join her with the sea.

S gropes the density of this *sense*. S knows that the direction that Phaon's body is facing (away from her) *is* Phaon's current erection.

Her understanding of the catastrophe of the loss in her body rings and Aphrodite rides the ringing further into S.

"You have what you have built, Sappho. You have the love and devotion of your women, and you have what you have constructed for Cleis. Nothing is lost."

"Sweet Cleis!" S exclaims softly, with an exhale, as she feels herself returning to her body, more solidified than before, as she gains composure on the edge of the cliff.

Is one encounter with *else* enough to change your whole life?

Awareness of her daughter momentarily sobers her; a jubilant jouissance deluges her body. When she remembers Cleis' young cries as an infant, a juicy rush of lactation swells in her nipples and fills her up.

This unintended engorgement by *memory as body* reminds her of Phaon's full body erection. Her back arches and her chest opens to the still-storming sky.

It is at this moment of somatic abundance that S slips off the ledge.

So many years after her death, an auricular-judae (creamy looking, linen-like, reddish mushroom) begins to grow on the base of a statue of Sappho. The mushroom seems to become more abundant every time a storm arises. Soon, local lovers of the statue begin to notice that the mushroom's abundance has covered the entire base of the statue.

Conversation ensues about whether the *distributing feral* should be removed from the shrine. The locals and the lovers decide to sleep on the consideration. It storms all through the night. In the morning, when they re-approach the statue, the smell of petrichor and decay overwhelms. There are enormous fissures all the way through the statue and as it fills them, mushroom-fecundity is increasing the size of those splits.

Within hours, the statue of Sappho is subsumed in carmine, buttery tone. The engorging mushroom overtakes the once-gleaming and polished marble of S' *first* form.

All of Sappho's fragments which appear as underlined phrases in the book are quoted from either of these locations:

http://www.gutenberg.org/files/12389/12389-8.txt

http://www.poetryintranslation.com/PITBR/Greek/Sappho.htm

www.ingramcontent.com/pod-product-compliance
Lightning Source LLC
Chambersburg PA
CBHW041130110526
44592CB00020B/2752